C000150466

POIGNANT LANDSCAPES

POIGNANT LANDSCAPES

Reflections on pain, beauty, belonging,
and being human

Van Thi Diep

A FLOURISHING
COMMONS

Part of the essay "The Void" was originally published in a different version as "The Landscape of the Void: Truth and Magic in Chinese Landscape Painting", *Journal of Visual Arts Practice*, Vol. 16, Issue 1, 2017, pp. 77-86. Re-used with permission from Taylor & Francis Group (https://www.tandfonline.com).

Cover design and interior photographs by the author
Published by A Flourishing Commons
www.flourishingcommons.com

Ebook ISBN: 978-1-7381033-0-0
Paperback ISBN: 978-1-7381033-1-7
Hardcover ISBN: 978-1-7381033-2-4

To the poignant
landscapes that warm my
heart, the trees that listen
to my dreams and sorrows,
and the flowers that teach
me how to bloom.

CONTENTS

INTRODUCTION

This book is a collection of essays, poems, and photographs that span nearly three decades, documenting my journey to seek the meaning of the poignant landscapes in my life. In this journey, I discovered that the secret to landscape's power is its ability to work incognito: to be formless but disguised as materiality, to transcend the walls between inner and outer nature, and to connect the paradox of what is known with the unknown with ease. Protected from the human ego's need for certainty, poignant landscapes speak through language, imagery, embodiment, and raw emotions. Although forever ambiguous and mysterious, all I need is a poignant landscape to remind me of my existential belongingness, because in this encounter, I inevitably become moved by my existence in the world.

Similarly ambiguous and illusory are our lives as human beings. To be human in the world with other humans, however, means to adopt an intermediary narrative tool. But unlike the poignant landscapes that simply remind me that I belong, in the world of humans, I must sieve through the mediating narratives to arrive at my own belonging. These narratives weave in and out of consciousness, like a woven tapestry, so different from the straightforward explanations found in textbooks that simplify what we know about the world, or the neat and linear lists found in resumes that simplify what we believe to be worthy about ourselves. Our mind's relationship with time further complicates this tapestry: on one hand, desiring to see time as linear and chronological, while on the other hand, time-travelling to the past and the future in ruminations and worries. To reflect the elusiveness of our interwoven consciousness, this book also weaves in and out of poetry, prose, and imagery. Intercepting my more recent reflections is a section in the middle called "Does Time Exist?" which includes a few pieces of writing by my teenage self, who also wanted to be witnessed here to show that the search for belonging transcends our usual limited sense of time.

Contrary to Capitalist-Cartesian logic and the belief that quantity equals value and more explanation equals greater clarity, I've decided to keep the book short and the essays concise, to trust in your intuitive ability to read between the lines and find resonance in the space between the pages of my semi-fragmented contemplations. From ecology to aesthetics to spirituality, in-between spaces are often described as places of opportunity. For example, the Chinese character for in-between (*jiān*) illustrates the sun between doors, portraying a threshold of a new beginning. The same character in Japanese (*ma*) is the negative space of consciousness: the silence that speaks. Similarly, ecotones are transitional areas between two biological communities, often holding more biodiversity than the habitats they integrate. In a cultural rite of passage, liminality is the place of non-status and ultimate equality.[1] And at a cosmic level, the Void is the originator of all things in Daoism. Poignant landscapes, for me, are also experienced in moments when in-between states of being in the world are made visibly meaningful.

Since many of the essays originated as excerpts from my PhD dissertation, you will find references to comments by landscape architects whom I interviewed or surveyed for my research.

Because of the interdisciplinary and existential nature of my dissertation, I like to describe it as a study of three intertwining narratives: a narrative of me and my life (a personal story); a narrative of humanity (a collective story of what it means to be human in the world); and an anecdotal narrative of how the first two stories become manifested in the world through a profession called landscape architecture. While these three narratives cover different scales of being, they arise from the same theme: finding home or belongingness in the world. My personal story is one about learning to overcome insecurity and discovering how to feel at home in myself; the collective story is one about humanity's struggle to feel belonging in nature, *as part of* nature, in a greater universe; and lastly, the one about landscape architecture is a story about a group of humans whose role is to "make place" in this world. The research ideas used to evoke this shared storytelling were the interpretations of what makes landscape poignant and what makes humans flourish.

However, this book is not about landscape architects or landscape architecture. As a reader, you don't need to be interested or associated with the profession. But since *place* and *belonging* at the emotional and spiritual levels are interchangeable, in the context of human flourishing, we are all *place-makers*—meaning that in archetypal form, any one of us can resonate with the landscape architect's dilemma in relating to landscapes, human systems, and the ontological need to create space for belonging. You may also be familiar with the following scenarios distilled from my research as potential characteristics for a poignant landscape experience: feeling wholly immersed in a place; opening to the awareness that one is part of a greater nature; noticing elements in nature that have been taken for granted; being emotionally moved by how one's actions have affected others; and being aware of non-connection, placelessness, or not-belonging.

The last scenario for a poignant landscape experience reveals that pain does not need to be separate from the journey to true belonging. Moreover, pain is often a necessary part of the self-actualization process. Therefore, I often describe poignant to be the moment when pain meets beauty. For collective consciousness, poignant is also the juncture between the shadows of our humanity and the realization of our inherent belongingness in the world. And so, to truly flourish means to understand and embody this belonging as physical and spiritual beings.

In the metaphor of flourishing, a cycle starts from the potentiality held within a seed. So perhaps, you could say that I had been collecting the seeds for this book from my earliest days as a landscape architecture student to my more recent days as a doctoral researcher in phenomenology. But while much of these insights germinated at a place of intellectualism (physically, in a university, and conceptually, from thinking), this book is not intended for the intellectual. This book and whatever seeds of potential it carries are meant for the *warrior* with the courage to feel and the *lover* who is idealistic enough to surrender. That is because to have faith in our belonging requires us to trust our inner knowing—to respect the fact that knowledge gained through external sources is not more valuable than personal wisdom, even if our social systems say otherwise. Yet, this challenge is one of our biggest impediments to overcome because even if landscapes don't judge us, we humans have mastered the ability to judge landscapes, judge each other, and judge ourselves before we can even attempt to seek the truth of who we are.

However, the lesson in learning to accept that some structures are open to change and disturbance while others are stubbornly resistant is not easy. But the outcome of this lesson, from my experience, is the ability to discern the fertile environments, for which the seeds of the heart can grow, from the barren environments that leave no potential to sustain the love of life. However, the first environment we must tend to is the one inside ourselves. Therefore, the commitment to unconditional belonging is simultaneously a path toward overcoming pain, finding a home within ourselves, and sharing the beauty of what makes life worthwhile with each other.

In nurturing our individual sense of belonging in the world, we are also naturally contributing to the healing of our collective traumas. As an intuitive empath who can feel the pain of the world so viscerally within my mental and somatic awareness, the journey to self-belonging has been longwinded, to say the least. But at every intermission of this journey, I find myself returning to the same profoundly healing message. In a poignant landscape, I am told that I deserve to exist in the world. And so too does everyone else. In the gratitude of receiving our landscapes' loving message is also the trust that I am here to share this message with you.

The Language of Landscapes

LANGUAGE, LANDSCAPES, AND BEING IN THE WORLD

Poignant is one of my favourite words in the English language. Perhaps I am charmed by how the word disobeys the simplicity of the alphabet's phonetic decoding. Or perhaps, I am enchanted by the thought of its silent "g" and invisible "y" conspiring together to persuade me that there is magic to language. When I enunciate the word *poignant*, I am transported into a pool of emotions. These emotions exist without language, and yet language opens the door to an intuitive way of being in the world.

On a planet full of anxious humans and social-ecological issues, poignant landscapes whisper to me that there are no problems to solve, only mysteries to unconceal. That is because a problem, according to French philosopher Gabriel Marcel, is something that we encounter outside of us that is ready to be reduced, but a mystery is something that we are involved in that we cannot be distinctly separated from.[2] So in the acknowledgement of our interconnectedness with the world, what else is there except for mysteries? In the case of poignant landscapes, they are mysteries because my affinity to them cannot be split into two distinct parts: me and landscape. A poignant landscape is a landscape that embodies what the word *poignant* means, and to me, *poignant* is a word that expresses a non-linguistic way of being in the world. *Poignant* is conceptually ambiguous, and as such, epitomizes the mystery of being human in a complex world.

For many years, I deeply wanted others to resonate with my passion for poignant landscapes. At one time, as a landscape architect, I secretly judged the profession of landscape architecture. I questioned why landscape architects, presumedly, did not care if the landscapes around us were not poignant. I wondered why landscape architects, presumably, did not intend to create landscapes that were poignant. But as much as I wanted everyone to think, make, and dream poignant landscapes, I knew deep inside me that this universal revelation was not possible. Or at least not in the way I had initially thought it to be.

Frankly, I did not know at the time what poignant landscapes really meant to me. What I did know was that I had the habit of yearning to find the feeling of a poignant landscape in an actual experience. A view of Lake Louise in Banff National Park; hiking up Mount Misen in Miyajima, Japan; waking up to the Alps of Switzerland on a tour bus; the stillness of an inlet on an Alaskan cruise in front of a glacier; all were beautiful landscapes that I had the chance to experience. While they were almost poignant, they were not the poignant landscape experience I was looking for. My yearning felt similar to a pilgrimage, but I did not know exactly my pilgrimage destination. Now I know that the real pilgrimage that was waiting for me all along was the journey into myself.

Pilgrimages are often taken with religious intentions. So even though I do not subscribe to any religion, as a philosopher in phenomenology, my work is without a doubt an undertaking into spirituality. However, words related to spirituality, or more accurately, words related to religion, can bring about much contention. I recall early in my doctoral studies saying to an advisor, "I think I need to talk about God. How can I talk about nature and the sublime in Western history without talking about God? But I don't think 'people' will like it if I do." Whether these "people" were real future critics or imaginary voices in my mind, it didn't matter. The choice to use particular words was intimidating.

I don't remember my advisor's answer, but he must have responded encouragingly because as my studies progressed, I got a little braver to use words deliberately yet not too prudently. Now, I choose to use triggering words like *God* intentionally. In the case of *God* as a word and a concept, there is an association with a holy figure as well as an association with the hermeneutic irony of our human existence to all else—our histories and our cultures (i.e., religion, science, and ideologies), the relationship to ourselves (i.e., faith and reason), and the nature around us. There is no other word, let it be the divine, the sublime, the sacred, or the magical, that embodies the impenetrable power and cultural conflict that the word *God* carries with it.

Just like *God*, all words can have multiple associations and interpretations. Just like *poignant*, all words have the potential to trigger emotions and shape our intuitive non-linguistic understanding of the world. But if landscape and language are foundational to making place and being in the world, and if communication is interpretative and experiences are subjective, how can a person advocate for the appreciation of...well...anything? How can we influence someone's experience in a landscape or otherwise with intention? To clarify, I'm not talking about the "experience" that we can report on or choreograph. The kind of experience I'm referring to is lived experience. While we cannot truly know someone else's experience because we cannot live out anyone else's experience other than our own, there is one thing we can still do: share the stories of our experiences so that we can learn more about each other. Therefore, language is what mediates our personal experiences with our collective existence as a linguistic species.

Just as I have an affinity for poignant landscapes, I've been learning that I also have an affinity for storytelling. I wanted others to be fascinated by poignant landscapes so that I could collect their stories of poignant experiences and be moved by their experiences of the world. I also wanted people to be moved by their own stories and each other's stories but since research in the academic tradition is more than an assemblage of stories, I needed to learn how to create value out of my heart's yearnings. So, in the process of returning back to the magic of language to see that research is also to *re*-search, I realized that what I sought may also have been something that I (and we) already know.

What I've been searching for in my personal yearning for emotional resonance with others, perhaps, was a self-discovery that is simultaneously collective: the confirmation that our lives, played out in our experiences and our relationship with the world, do matter. And amidst personal and collective apprehension, confusion, apathy, or trauma, there is still an essence to being human that is worth living for.

THE GIFT OF LANGUAGE

If words are our humanly gift to the world,
Why is writing so difficult?
I struggle to piece together
What I genuinely want to say
So that you can understand my heart.
But why am I here
If I cannot give back the gift that I've been blessed with?
I can only say that I'll give it a try,
To learn to love to write
So that the love I've been blessed with
Is shared and reciprocated.

A PROBLEM WITH LANDSCAPES

A landscape architect with many years of professional and life experience told me in a research interview that "the word landscape is not a very good one." He said, "Landscape is often used to talk about environment... [but] most people...see cities and landscape as opposites." In this assertion, I extracted several common assumptions: some people don't see landscapes as urban, some people don't see cities as landscapes, and landscapes are not necessarily the same as environment. These assumptions are true in that there is variability in how people see landscapes, yet the opposites to these assumptions are also true: some people do see landscapes as urban, some people do see cities as landscapes, and landscapes can be interpreted as our environments.

Within the discourse of landscape with landscape architects was a conundrum: in every sentence, landscape implied something, and oftentimes that something was a notion that the speaker wanted to advocate against in landscape thought. A research participant said, "I worked in a nursery, digging trees, and being right at the earth [...] So that's not a landscape." And, "there have been some pretty neat sunsets...now, they are not landscapes." Another person said, "I don't know if you grew up in a landscape too." Another one said, "If you don't see how humans fit in that natural landscape, that's not being a landscape architect." And another, "When I say landscape architecture, I don't mean just the designed places or the urban places. For me, landscape architecture is also the wild places."

Almost everyone in the environmental studies or landscape design professions would nod in approval to the movement to dismantle the nature-culture binary. Yet these examples show how language would betray our intentions: landscape is not a human activity; landscape is not an astronomical phenomenon; one can grow up not in a landscape; a category of landscapes that is considered natural exists, but many humans don't see themselves as part of; and designed landscapes are synonymous to urban landscapes but not wild landscapes. Of course, I am not immune to this conundrum of language. Even if I tried to consciously avoid the trap of contradictory meanings with words such as *landscape* and *nature* in my writing, as a social being conditioned by language, I would still have difficulty curbing these inconsistencies all the time. Therefore, every instance of the word *landscape* can imply a constructed meaning that may also challenge another meaning.

Perhaps, *landscape* is indeed a problem. But the predicament of *landscape* is not because there is a better word to replace it. Instead, the predicament is created because language does not have the capacity to carry the weight of what landscape is meant to mean. Language represents the perceived world, but certain things that are seemingly invisible can become visible when they are perceived in a different way. For example, wind is invisible to the eye, but we hear it and see its effect on other objects. Similarly, light is intangible, and yet we cannot see anything else without it. Landscape is affective precisely because of this resistance to being represented by language.[3] On one hand, landscape is about material entities—tangible and real—while on the other hand, landscape is about meaning and cultural ideologies—intangible, fluid, and formless. Landscape can span across two, three, and four dimensions, and can morph to whatever form we would like it to take on.

Originally, we are told that the word *landscape*, deriving from the Dutch word *landschap*, was used to describe administrative units of farm fields,[4] but as paintings of these fields arose in the 16th century, the term became associated with the representation of land and nature. Today, landscape can be described as synonymous with scenery, but landscape imagery as scenery goes all the way back to the backgrounds of Greek and Roman theatres.[5] Accordingly, if landscapes were stage backgrounds to theatrical performances, then metaphorically, landscapes can also be interpreted as the backdrops to life's performances. Hence, landscape as a metaphorical product of the conceptual split between humans and our environments is not only a historical-cultural narrative, landscape also reveals a story of humanity's relationship with our world. This story is parallel to our self-created story of nature.

In mainstream cultures, nature is told as a complex and disjointed story. Sometimes nature is described as separate from human civilization, for example, the "wilderness" is considered a place where people extract time from their busy lives to learn about nature or to relax in it. Sometimes, nature is described as fragments of wilderness found in human environments, for example, urban forests or songbirds in cities. At other times, nature is described as elements that are tended to by humans such as animals on a farm or plants in a garden. In landscape architecture, sometimes the goal is to work with nature, while other times, landscape's automatic association with nature becomes misleading because a lot of the work does not include typical "natural" living elements. Although there is no consensus on what nature is and how nature shapes landscape architecture, I found that in our use of language, nature is generally perceived as something that each person "relates" to. How a person relates to nature is shaped by how nature has shown up in their experiences of the world.

One way that nature shows up in our world regardless of where we are is through language. How we interpret nature is how we interpret ourselves as human beings. If nature is considered purely a resource used for commodities, human beings become consumers who deplete natural resources. If nature is considered a luxury, then only certain humans are worthy of nature's comfort. If nature is considered an enemy, then humans respond to the threat by domination and control. If nature is considered kin, humans become part of an ecological community. If nature is considered home, then humans belong in it.

Landscapes are the stories of these interpretations of nature that get relived through experience. The power of landscape is found in the visible and invisible layers of natural and social processes coming together in a personal experience. The profoundness of a poignant landscape experience illustrates how nature, culture, place, and time are part of a bigger cosmology that can be palpably found embodied in one singular landscape. This landscape mirrors back to us how humans play roles in the world as ecological, social, and spiritual participants. So while putting a definition to the word *landscape* may be difficult because of its ambiguity, finding meaning in landscapes is not all that difficult; so much that meanings found in landscapes are so complex that simple definitions for nature, culture, place, and time are insufficient.

Our fascination with human history and landscape's legacy shows that place-making, or more broadly, human belongingness in the world, is fundamentally important to the meaning of landscapes. Since place-making is dependent on the interpretation of our human-world relationship, place-making is also a process of evaluating how we want to participate in our world. Do we want to be apathetic? Do we want to be disheartened? Do we want to be fearful? Or do we want to be enchanted by the world? If the choice is enchantment, then I suggest that interpreting what makes landscapes poignant is a good place to start.

WHEN PAIN MEETS BEAUTY

POIGNANT HAPPENS WHEN PAIN MEETS BEAUTY

I've come to realize that the world we live in has been wounded for a very long time. We enter this world also somewhat wounded and beneath everyday routines is a layer of pain. Nobody is "immune" to this pain,[6] yet to fully accept it can be difficult because humans generally desire happiness and avoid sadness. A scene from the Pixar animation *Inside Out* (2015) demonstrates this phenomenon fittingly, as Joy, the emotion, insists on keeping Sadness, another emotion, inside a bounded circle to keep their human girl happy.

Then again, sadness is not the only emotion that is habitually denied by the modern human. I would say that emotions in general were never fully welcomed as part of the development of modern human civilization. Since the Middle Ages shifted into the Renaissance, Western culture has prized the thinking mind over sentimentality. And for only a relatively brief period in the last 600 years or so of modernity has emotionality prevailed over reasoning in a major cultural movement (i.e., Romanticism from c.1770-1850). Not surprisingly, the fascination with nature also accompanied this time of emotional exploration because feelings are also part of human nature.

Still, even if the mind is in control, it does not mean emotions are non-existent. Instead, these difficult emotions are repressed in our subconscious minds and bodies. Of course, repressing emotions has consequences. A society of humans with repressed emotions can foster nihilism and a collective inability to participate in authentic and healthy culturing.[7] Therefore, the nature-culture binary may not inherently exist, but in the mass fear of our own emotions, the binary becomes a self-fulfilling prophecy. Furthermore, in a patriarchal-leaning society, emotions, nature, and femininity are exiled together to create a world where nature has no self-authority,[8] femininity is devalued, and emotions are scary.

Ecopsychology scholar and retired psychotherapist Andy Fisher notes the absurdity of how contemporary society treats mental disorders, that is, having individuals appear at therapist offices to get analyzed over their independent life stories and traumas while the social forces that brought them there continue to create violence, destruct the biosphere, and perpetuate the supply of more wounded souls.[9] This cycle of collective social violence almost seems inevitable, but the notion of poignancy offers me more than a glimmer of hope.

My intention in using the word *poignant* in my research was to inspire a discourse on the power of landscapes through the evocative emotions of landscape experiences. However, *poignant* contains elements of sadness, and as mentioned earlier, sadness is not the usual welcomed guest in social systems that have been traditionally patriarchal, such as academia and professional associations. For instance, a research participant told me that they preferred to use the word *uplifting* because poignant had "a little too much sadness to it." Hearing this, I was almost ready to abandon *poignant* for something more "uplifting" so that I could continue to inspire others through landscapes, but in my reaffirmed commitment to *poignant* and its wisdom, I discovered a revelation about human suffering. Poignant moments that arise from difficult life experiences must have elements of pain.

The etymology of the word *poignant* reveals a long history of being associated with sudden and painful experiences: the 14th century Latin word *pungere*, meaning to prick or pierce, or the 13th century French term *poindre* and its present participle *poignant,* meaning things sharp and pointed that prick.[10] Mysteriously, *poignant* is also used to describe scenarios that are beautifully painful. So, although the combination of beauty and pain can be somewhat of an oxymoron, if we consider pain as the suffering that life offers for growth, beauty can find its way in as a type of healing process.

Therefore, poignant moments are the moments when suffering becomes awareness, and perhaps, even the awareness of the world's absurdity. In these moments, beauty shows itself as wounds heal. To deny pain means to deny the poignant. To deny the poignant means to deny the beauty of healing. To deny the beauty of healing means to deny life itself. But this life-affirming beauty must be more than skin-deep. Beauty that can heal a society's greatest wounds needs to come from something even greater than society itself. Only when creation, destruction, intimacy, and hate are considered parts of a greater cosmological structure, can the pain and beauty of life co-exist together.

JEWELED TEARS

A fountain of tears
Where do they come from?
They flow as if there is an infinite source of pain
That wants to become jewels
Sparkling
Nourishing
Transforming into all that is beautiful in the world.

POIGNANT LANDSCAPES TELL US THAT WE BELONG

Large numbers of people in the world are immigrants. People relocate their homes for employment, for their children's future, or for lifestyle changes. People also relocate in order to flee disasters, oppression, or violence. Therefore, the idea of home doesn't necessarily mean a place of permanence. We strive to make the place we live in become home. Yet, to feel totally *at home* within a place is not all that common in our present-day world. We are almost always seeking a mythical home elsewhere...an ideal in the past, in the future, or in another dimension. The need to transcend to another world is the tension between the need to find home and the inability to feel at home exactly where we are.

According to spiritual activist and teacher Stephen Jenkinson, human populations historically "wandered" across the planet: from Africa, along the coasts of the Middle East and South Asia, into Australia; following the mountains across Asia to the Americas; and along the coasts of the Mediterranean into and around Europe.[11] These ancestral nomads did not move because they were forced to, but instead, they "collaborated" with the places they lived in. They moved with the wind, the water, and the animals. Or in other words, they belonged with the Earth's processes. In contrast, as Jenkinson states, there is a difference between wandering and fleeing. Fleeing is the state of being forced from the land and the possessions one calls home, while wandering is a state of totally being at home in the world without the need for possessions and an attachment to a plot of land. Nevertheless, being at home in the world requires the feeling of belonging, whether that be to a community, to the land, to the Earth, to the universe, or simply, to oneself.

Belongingness requires a certain level of sensitivity to the elements in the place that we belong to. This may mean nurturing the acceptance of our thoughts, emotions, and physical bodies when we belong to ourselves; the people around us when we belong to a community; the human and more-than-human beings that exist when we belong to the Earth; and to the tangible and intangible forces of life and death when we belong to the universe. Yet paradoxically, as humans, we have the tendency to craft rigid judgments of what should be in a place, who should be in a place, and how to control a place, disregarding the fact that what is *supposedly natural* is always a fluid and interrelated process.

As a research participant once told me, we bring our landscapes with us when we move from one place to another. These landscapes may be physical plants or may be visions of what brings us comfort. In his words, we are the "operations of nature." As we change, nature changes too. Therefore, arguments about "living with nature" are usually made with too little nuance. One area of contention is the native/non-native plant discourse in environmental design and management. Doubting my intuition, I once thought the discursive link between plant belonging and human belonging could just be a metaphorical leap in my own mind, but hearing the topic of non-native *plants* emerge from other people's mouths in personal conversations about *human* belonging suggests that the association may be part of a larger collective cognitive dissonance we have about what it means to belong as natural beings on Earth.

As a thought exercise, I have asked myself if I was metaphorically a plant, would I be dismissed in landscape designs due to my non-native status? Or does having lived decades in Canada enough to be "naturalized" as a "Canadian plant"? But what about my parents who have never managed to "naturalize" and adapt to the English language or to many North American standards? What about new immigrants who come into a country? More broadly, can we ever find home if belonging to a place has to be tied to where we were born, where our genetic ancestors resided, or even where our physical residence is located?

Fortunately, our relationship with landscapes can transcend the judgements of social discourse. As humans, we have opportunities to feel belonging even in places outside of our usual residence. For example, one landscape architect I interviewed recalled how her acquaintance found healing in the landscapes of Nova Scotia despite being a resident of Waterloo, Ontario. She had initially dismissed her acquaintance's interest in coastal landscapes but had been humbled in the conversation when she realized that poignant landscape experiences are not bound by human-constructed jurisdictions. Instead, these landscapes speak to people's emotions.

Another story that this research participant shared was the time when she was trapped in rural Labrador for work during the 9/11 terrorist attack. Satellite communication to the region was shut off shortly after the community had seen CNN coverage of the collapsing World Trade Towers. In those moments of not knowing what was going on with the rest of the world, and not knowing if she would be able to see her loved ones again, the need for home was profound. The awareness of one's place in the world was even greater. The experience was described as poignant because within her dread was also love and compassion. The Naskapi Innu community had taken her in for the evening and in the morning, she was accompanied on foot for hundreds of kilometres along the coast of Labrador to a port where she was able to take a ship home to her extended family in Gander, Newfoundland.

In this story, to yearn for home in a frightening situation was poignant. In the previous story, to be healed in a landscape was poignant. Both experiences happened in places where the individuals felt belonging. In the reciprocal relationship of being embraced by a landscape—of humans and non-humans, without judgment—a poignant landscape experience mirrors an awareness of finding home and belonging in the world: from the desire for place, to fearing placelessness, and eventually, to finding belongingness as a person within a landscape.

Most of us, if not all humans, want to make the place we are in become home, figuratively, whether that is a transient place to heal, or a stable place to grow roots. And for certain, there is one home we all share: Planet Earth. Therefore, the quintessential home that human beings want to belong to is our earthly home and our worthy existence as human beings in this home. Finding home requires us to feel welcomed and to be supported. Being at home requires us to feel that we have a right to exist. Yet, if we find ourselves in societies devoid of authenticity, if economic growth is valued over emotional and spiritual growth, and if every person who looks or thinks differently is considered an "other," the seeds of belonging have little room to grow.

Yet, in the context of home being a sense of belonging, poignant landscapes are the experiences that remind us that we indeed do always belong. In comparison to this existential message of us belonging to life, our human judgments and limitations on belonging become merely the distortions of misinterpreted child's play. Placelessness and non-belonging are healed through the beauty of knowing that we inherently belong as part of a community, a society, and more importantly, as human beings in a cosmological structure that is much greater than us. Those seeds of belonging had always been naturally planted within us all along.

THE NIGHT-SEA JOURNEY
BACK HOME

Carl Jung considered the journey into the underworld (*nekyia*) or the night-sea journey as the analogy of a person's venture into the psyche's deep unconscious.[12] The rejected parts of the psyche, that is our shadows, live in these recesses. But to James Hillman, this journey into the underworld is not synonymous with the night-sea journey.[13] In the underworld, according to Hillman, the visitor becomes subsumed by the devil, that is, fear, shame, and guilt continue to linger in the shadows. Yet, in a night-sea journey, the protagonist gains strength by their victory against the sea monster.

If the immensity of our world's social-ecological issues is our psyches calling out from the shadows of our collective unconscious, then who are the sea monsters? What if our attempts to critique, analyze, and fix our (world) problems are merely the chasing of our shadows? In water, lighthouses guide mariners on their night-sea journeys toward a safe return home. On land, we venture into a dark forest with a flashlight. Therefore, regardless of what monsters lurk within the shadows, in times of despair, we also need a light source that celebrates the beauty of life.

In the darkness of our shadows, poignant landscapes become navigating signposts to our existential home on Earth because they allow us to be moved by the world. Our memories of the poignant experiences we've had tell us that we are part of a greater world in which we belong. These experiences can mean a variety of potential situations: awe, curiosity, gratitude, serenity, or even shame and fear. Even the experiences of pain reveal a silver lining: in the poignant image of the night-sea journey lit by moonlight, we win over the sea monster within ourselves to find our way back home.

Finding home

What is home?
They say that home is where the heart is
So are our hearts broken
When finding home becomes so difficult?

A place to be me
When can I let go of the burdens I carry?
Of the past
From before I was even born,
Of the present
In loyalty to other people's pain,
Of the future
That has not yet been formed.

But it's already there
This home
In my heart, and in yours
It can never be taken away
By landlords, property taxes, and bulldozers
I know it, and you know it too
It's calling for our return.

Our hearts are waiting
Wounded, but not broken
The path is open
To return home.

A PHILOSOPHY FOR WHY WE ARE THE WAY WE ARE

I find social identity labels troublesome. These labels don't usually explain who I really am, and yet they give people—or worse, myself—the impression of who I *should* be. Do I choose to lose myself in trying to fit into a label by becoming an imposter who abandons my true self to belong somewhere in other people's eyes? Or do I risk my chance of not being seen at all? So when I do choose a label for myself, I'm left with conflicting statements of identity. Yet, at the end of the day, I'm just ME, no more and no less.

If anything, I would consider myself a philosopher. But there is something weird about calling yourself a philosopher in the modern world...unless you look like Dumbledore...or believe that you are a reincarnation of Aristotle, Lao Tzu, Descartes, Kant, Nietzsche, etc....or at the very least, you teach philosophy at a university. But by committing to this stereotype, I'd be leaving out most of the population eligible to be philosophers. So even though no legal or ethical restrictions surround the philosopher title, and even though I have a Doctor of Philosophy and a "love for wisdom," I still feel awkward using the philosopher title in professional settings.

Outside of academia, many people see philosophy as superfluous—a luxury that brings nothing of value other than intellectual entertainment. On the other hand, there are people within academia who would dissect a philosopher's text like specimens under a microscope. Conversations based on arguments and counterarguments of philosophical ideas or attempts to prove the correct perspective of a philosopher's intent were things I witnessed and even participated in, but I've wondered, what is the point of all this? Is this kind of philosophy an intellectual sport or is this rational examination of what one Great Philosopher said supposedly going to reveal a universal truth about the world so that we can bring in world peace and a loving society?

Certainly, in the writings of many Great Philosophers are wonderful advice about creating personal peace and happiness, but to believe that anyone other than myself would think that philosophy could have the answers to our world's "problems" was my own oversimplification about what life-changing philosophy demands of us. As a communication tool, philosophy relies on logic and rationality, but as a personal exercise, my motive to be philosophical is emotional. In my own personal environmental philosophy, I know that human beings have an intrinsic connection to nature because we are also nature; we want to belong on this planet, and we want to make home of our lives on this planet; and yet, collectively, we are so far off from this perfect harmony of "home-sweet-home."

I turn to philosophy so that I can find reasons to why we are the way we are. I need these reasons because I feel the pain when I see humans harming other humans, let alone when we do not care for our own home. I turn to spirituality because I feel the pain when I believe I know the reasons why we are the way we are as human beings and watch the train wreck happen regardless. Despite my eagerness to share what I know so that we can change, I encounter what I perceive as resistance from those who are oblivious to these reasons and are reluctant to reflect on them. Then I need further reasons to know why this resistance is also the way we are.

The final conclusion of my inquiry: that is just the way we are. There are people here on Earth to maintain existing conditions. There are people here on Earth to make life a challenge for others. There are people here on Earth who find existing conditions and challenging people or circumstances hard to bear and choose to act towards some change. And lastly, there are people here on Earth who are meant to find out that real change happens internally first.

We come into the world to learn, to distill, and to embody our own truth, so we are always our own philosophers. Your personal philosophy will tell you which one of these people you are meant to be.

Does Time Exist?

UNDER THE SKY, UP IN THE MOUNTAINS, LOST IN TIME

Under the big sky, the feeling of being human is inevitable because the human body is scaled in relation to the rest of the world. Simultaneously limited and earthbound, under the vastness of the sky, humans are made aware that we are connected to something much greater than ourselves. As Martin Heidegger has said, humans have "always measured [ourselves] with and against something heavenly"; even if we build skyscrapers to "block this spanning, trim it, and disfigure it...[we] can never evade it."[14]

On Earth, the sky connects humans to greater natural processes. The two sources of life, water and light, both come from the sky. Rain and sunlight nourish life on Earth as part of natural processes that are outside of human intervention. At night, the sky is Earth's window to the greater cosmos. In mythology and religion, the sky is heaven and home to the deities. But even without mythical or religious references to spirits, angels, gods, and goddesses, a clear night sky still alludes to an expansive universe with the presence of glittering moonlight, stars, and planets. Human-made light has made this capacious scene obsolete in urban regions, but the affection for the night sky's cosmic portal is primordial.

The sky is a measuring tool for an unknown realm. The feeling of connectedness with the sky is a state that exists between humbleness and potentiality. Children, who are more open in their understanding of what it means to be in the world, who are freer to use their imaginations in relation to the natural world than adults, recognize their connection to the sky intuitively as they engage in cloud watching. Most of us can likely recall a childhood experience of fantasizing about another world from the shapes of floating clouds. But those of us challenged with the retrieval of our forgotten childhood innocence can still reach the sky and dance among the clouds by finding our way up into the mountains.

Artists throughout centuries have been intrigued by mountains and similar landscapes that display expansive heights such as canyons, valleys, and fjords. These typologies have even become psychological icons for the landscapes of their corresponding nations, for example, the mountains hidden among mists in traditional Chinese landscape paintings, the rustic mountains painted by Dutch master Jacob van Ruisdael (1628-1682), and the nostalgic renditions of the Norwegian fjords by Hans Dahl (1849-1937). In the United States, Yosemite Valley was featured in numerous paintings by Albert Bierstadt (1830-1902), prompting the establishment of the US National Park System,[15] as well as in Ansel Adam's (1902-1984) evocative photographs for Sierra Club campaigns. In Canada, the Group of Seven's Lawren Harris (1885-1970) brought prominence to the country's northern landscapes, and those of us Canadians who have lived here for more than thirty years may still remember the image of Moraine Lake and its surrounding mountains featured on our twenty-dollar bills (from 1969 to 1993).

While seeing repetitive images of a certain landscape can influence how we appreciate a landscape,[16] mountains inherently hold significant symbology in the human psyche. Otherwise, we would not use the metaphor of climbing a mountain to describe the obstacles in life that need overcoming. Whether it is our ego's need to conquer the nature of our external and internal landscapes or reach the metaphorical summit of life to find greater connectedness with the cosmos, the mountain is an important archetype in our spiritual development. As a measure of geological, physical, and temporal magnitudes, mountains give scale to humanity's sense of hubris.

Mountains take a long time to form and are emblematic of the passing of eons, but elements in alpine ecosystems change seasonally. Similarly, the sky changes constantly as cloud formations shift and as the sun moves across it, yet the sky goes through daily, monthly, and annual cycles. Time becomes relational when we balance the fluid and cyclical processes of nature with the rigid schedules and timeframes of our human-constructed systems. The duration of human life becomes a limited perspective of time when we compare our ninety plus or minus years of existence to the timeframes of the world's natural landscapes. At the physical and temporal scales, human rationality is no measure to the other natural elements that have existed in our universe for much longer. Gratefully, in the wisdom of these landscapes, we can be reminded that we are merely here for just moments in time.

PAST PATH

Like walking through a painting
I see a calm, peaceful late summer day
The long green grass dances gently to the wind
As I follow the path which leads the way.

A path I have seen before
Maybe somewhere, sometime in the past
Beyond the green and purple shadowed bushes
I may find what I've been looking for, maybe, at last.

***

A poem found in a collection of old schoolwork. No date or grade was listed but considering that it was typed up and not handwritten (i.e., marking the evolution of humanity's dependency on the computer in parallel with the timeline of my youth), I assume it was written around the time I was 14 years old.

THE DIARY OF A PRE-TEEN PHILOSOPHER

Years ago, in an attempt to clean out the emotional baggage of my childhood, I threw away a bunch of old diaries from my pre-teen and teenage years. Cringing as I scanned through the entries before the pages were destroyed, I discovered that 1) I was capable of being very angry, a state that I increasingly repressed as I grew up; 2) I sometimes wrote and complained to God even though I was never religious; and 3) I had always been an existential philosopher. The only thing left from these diaries is the excerpt below, which I found amusing and endearing enough to keep as a photograph in commemoration:

> *I wonder why we are here. How do we know that there are other people in the world? We only know ourselves. To me, it's just a kind of dream that lasts for so long and anything can happen. In our dream, there's school, jobs, countries, beliefs, myths, everything. Well, after we die, we don't know if the world continues. Maybe the dream says there's Christmas and B.C., dinosaurs, cave people. How do we know they existed?*

Thirty years have passed, and while I may not have a clear answer for all the questions I had posed, my intuition and spiritual development can now offer some insights to reassure my younger self. I'd like to believe that other people do exist, and that the world will continue after I die, not because I know this to be absolutely true, but rather, because I know I exist *now*. In my own presence, I feel the presence of my fellow human beings, of the past, of the present, and of the future.

OUTSIDE

I open the window
To look outside,
But I find nothing there
Except the grey.

***

Another poem from my high school homework collection. Was I channeling my inner pessimist or just observing a normal November day in Toronto? Since I won't be able to get an answer from my younger self, I can only honour her by looking outside and appreciating the colours of the world, including the notorious urban grey.

I WONDER...

I wonder about the true importance of life. In life, a person is given tasks and risks to take, and for a reward, they will have something in life to enjoy. Sometimes, even after a storm, more storms will follow, whether we deserve a reward or not. To me, life can be wonderful if it was meant to be but appalling when a person ruins it.

To care for yourself is the first step in life. To care for others is the next. Without the first step, a person cannot go up the stairs of life. To succeed and to go up the steps, a person needs to see beyond the obvious, and the true importance of life and the future. Many people out in the world live a horrible life, but in their eyes that is not significant. They can be satisfied with what they have, while others fight for the better of the best. Sometimes we do not need the obvious and explicit things to keep us alive. The esoteric and hidden part of life may be the most important and the most worth living for. Food and shelter may be essential, but the most momentous ingredients are not those things but a life with conscience, hope, view, and action.

I think it would be better to be a human than to be me. I have to see and watch all that is happening in the world, but humans can escape it. After death, a person is gone but memories of life will be stored inside my body and will remain there forever. As everyone dies and leaves this forever-lasting dream, the world and the importance of life stay behind. Left behind to see the future, to hold the secrets of the world and the past, until someone dares to save and free this eternal lasting mind, is me.

***

A middle-school assignment to see the world from the perspective of Auguste Rodin's sculpture The Thinker.

RAINDROPS

Drip, drop
The sound of water dropping from the world above
Monotonously enters our ears.
The sky darkens, shielded by grey clouds
Panic, everyone reaches for umbrellas
Children groaning, running back home
Where light can live.

Drip, drop
Against the windowpane we hear.
Flowers reaching for a drink
Toddlers giggling, splashing puddles
We feel the freshness on our fingers
Everyone hopeful and knowing
The sun will return.

***

The last of three poems from my teenage self.

BETWEEN HEAVEN AND EARTH

THE VOID

There is a saying in Chinese to describe the most stunning and surreal landscapes. The phrase *rén jiān xiān jìng* (human between immortal border) describes a landscape that is as divine as the realm that borders between mortality and immortality. In the Western equivalent, this landscape is somewhere between the magical fairyland and the heavenly sublime. Chinese landscape paintings often depict this scenery: mountainous landscapes among the mists, analogous to a place between heaven and earth. These misty mountains aligned with the Buddhist and Daoist philosophers' search for temple sites deep in nature away from the city. As such, the Chinese landscape painter, according to art scholar Michael Sullivan, was a perpetual philosopher whose understanding of the world would only grow with age.[17]

As a landscape lover and philosopher, what could I learn from these landscapes that float between heaven and earth? How could these landscapes fill the gaps between landscape as language and landscape as material? Luckily, I found that this gap could be mediated by Martin Heidegger's interpretation of Being in his fourfold between the polarities of earth-sky and mortality-divinity.[18] At the centre of the fourfold is the Void. Clearly defined as the point of conjuncture, but ambiguous nonetheless, the Void is intangible and inaccessible using Cartesian logic. The Void is not nothing, but also hardly can be described as something...until a little shift in imagination takes over. Visualizing the fourfold pictorially in the air with the sky above and the earth below, and the axis of mortality and divinity along the horizon, I came across an insight of clarity. The Void was a landscape: the divine landscape that borders between mortality and immortality that can be embodied in *any* physical landscape that holds space for our time as humans here on Earth.

Heidegger uses the metaphor of a forest clearing to describe the Void.[19] The forest clearing as a metaphor for the unconcealed is considered a revealing of truth. This truth is not about finding a single absolute reality in the Western scientific sense, but rather a personal clarity and acceptance that within uncertainty is also truth itself. The difference between the dark forest and the clearing is what is concealed or unconcealed within our perception, but the forest exists regardless of whether we are among the trees or in the clearing.

This analogy becomes apparent to me every time I want to photograph a forest. I can see the trees and their components of leaves, branches, and bark; I can feel the ground and the soil beneath; I can hear the rustling of leaves or the sounds of animals. Yet, I cannot get a picture of the forest *landscape* until I reach the clearing. After training as a forest therapy guide, I've learned again the importance of clearings. In forest therapy, participants are offered opportunities to engage with the forest in sensory and embodied ways, followed by opportunities for participants to share with each other what they have noticed during their time alone. While a small path is enough for someone to engage in presence with the forest, without a clearing, there is no space to share our truths with each other.

The difference between the Chinese term for landscape, *fēng jǐng* (wind scene), and the Chinese term for landscape painting, *shān shuǐ hua* (mountain water picture), illustrates landscape's paradox: a cognitive shift happens between embodiment and representation. An embodied landscape is a view into the invisible, while the represented landscape is an image of the material. Both the Voids of our physical and psychological landscapes come from the realm of the invisible: the Void in our physical landscapes holds our existential presence in space and time while the Void in our psychological landscapes holds the oneness of our collective presence behind the fragmented narratives of our separate existences. Like the "mountain water" image, these Voids cannot be seen without a cognitive shift. This shift depends on the awareness that totality still exists beyond our limited perceptions and the intention to make space for the silence of our collective truth in between the noise of our human ego narratives.

THE GARDEN

Nature, especially in cities, shows up on maps as patches of green spaces among a pattern of grey urban fabric. But in our lived experience, nature is also found in street corridors, backyards, railway tracks, parking lots, grocery stores, and even in our bodies. Since our human minds and language systems do not like complexity, we often separate non-human nature from human-made systems with simple symbols of green and grey. The reference is used quite literally in infrastructure design: grey infrastructure for centralized human-engineered systems and green infrastructure for ecological systems. But from this metaphor of colour, to limit the world to green or grey is to be colour-blind to all the other colours in the world. Ultimately, we end up with a bunch of contradictions.

For example, stones along a riverbed, in various shades of grey and tones of other colours, are considered natural and attractive; a concrete planter in an urban plaza, which can also come in shades of grey or tones of other colours, is considered not natural and less appealing; the tree by the riverside and the tree in the planter are both supposedly "natural", but the tree in the planter has less chance of surviving because it has not been given optimal conditions to grow in. But if urban plazas were not considered as "grey spaces" and were treated as equally beneficial to what is considered "wild" nature, would landscape design change to accommodate the life of the urban tree? I'm not sure, but for certain, with little thought, we continuously use language to put up boundaries between nature shaped by nature and nature shaped by humans.

Gardens, however, exist in the liminal space between nature and humans, refusing to be split into two parts so easily. As a philosophical concept, the garden diffuses the mind's need to allocate landscapes into binary categories. Portrayed as paradisiac landscapes that "existed apart from human agency", according to anthropologist Norris Johnson, the Garden of the Sun (in the Epic of Gilgamesh) and the Garden of Eden in Genesis were neither wilderness nor cultivated lands.[20] These gardens were "holding" places for humans prior to their revival (for Gilgamesh) or their punishment (for Adam and Eve) into a world that needed culture as a taming of nature, especially, the taming of human nature. From this spiritual perspective, the garden is a type of "third" space.

Without the intervention from Gods, humans have continued to make our own gardens as in-between spaces for ourselves—as extensions of homes, as leisure spaces, and as private sanctuaries. The garden in Japanese terminology reveals the complex nature of this liminal space: *niwa* meaning a garden space adjacent to a residence, but also historically as a place for human activity; *shima* meaning a garden-like space, but also holding the meaning of an island.[21]

From the paradise garden that bridges heaven and earth to the courtyard between the public and the private, the garden is a dialectic synthesis that cannot be defined by binary notions of nature and culture, concealed and unconcealed, sacred and profane. The garden is the Zen kōan to the question, what is nature?[22] As with all kōans, in which a paradoxical riddle is used to reveal the inadequacy of logic to provoke the realization of life's greater truths, no true answer to the meaning of nature can come from the thinking mind. The truth of nature is found in experiencing it.

POIGNANT LANDSCAPES ARE FOR THOSE WHO BELIEVE

To come up with a research project about landscape architecture and use poignant landscapes as a subject matter indicated that I subconsciously believed that designing poignant landscapes was possible. Yet, the answers to a research survey question I asked on whether the profession of landscape architecture was succeeding in making poignant landscapes came out to be rather ambivalent. Believing that poignant landscapes had to be more natural than designed and that budget constraints and regulations inhibit the creation of meaningful and moving landscapes, survey participants had envisioned a status quo of landscape architecture that did not include poignant landscapes in their work.

Yet, most of the landscape architects I interviewed saw poignant landscape architecture as an inherent goal for the profession. They believed that poignant landscapes were integral to the pursuit of good landscape architecture because they interpreted poignancy in their own ways. Accordingly, since poignancy is interpretative, poignant landscape architecture also cannot have a design formula. So, despite my attempts to associate poignancy with physical landscapes, I knew that the physical world was not the main trigger that inspired a person to see a landscape as poignant.

Within me is an inner knowing that poignant landscapes come from the inside out. Just like how we can look into our distressed psyches to reveal the ruptures of society or look at our damaged external landscapes to reveal the disharmony of our collective psyches, our relationship to what is poignant can also reveal how we see ourselves in relation to the world.

Not surprisingly, what I would have considered to be my top three poignant landscape experiences before I started my doctoral studies were all fictional landscapes. The first landscape was my childhood encounter with God—the divinity in all things—in Canadian luminist painter Lucius O'Brien's *Sunrise on the Saguenay, Cape Trinity* (1880). The second landscape was the awe of seeing nature and culture united in an image of a beach house in my search for inspiration for a design and technology project in high school. And finally, the third landscape was the literary setting for Frances Hodgson Burnett's *The Secret Garden*. The story of *The Secret Garden* is alluring because it tells of children healing by spending time in nature. But what is particularly special for me about this story is the underlying metaphor that a secret garden resides in a person's heart. This metaphor is a prompt for some deep reflective questions:

> *How beautiful is my garden blooming? Have I buried the keys and neglected the garden due to fear and heartbreak? Or have I tended to it gently? What if I could open this garden to others and share its beauty? Or help another person nurture their own garden?*

If it's possible for our secret gardens to be nurtured and shared, then the role of poignant landscapes in landscape architecture is not fantasy nor indulgence. This process supports the flourishing of our secret inner and public outer gardens, both metaphorically and physically. But only we can, as individuals, choose the paradigm that allows for this flourishing. Our home in nature starts with our sense of self in our individual universes. This home is not built of trees, flowers, or stones, but rather the words we use to bring the magic of trees, flowers, and stones into each other's lives. Ultimately, whether we consider place-making through landscapes as a physical or emotional endeavour, I can only be certain of one characteristic necessary for poignant landscape architecture. All the stories that I had gathered about poignant landscapes were humbling experiences, so accordingly, I'm sure that poignant landscape architecture and its archetypal equivalent of bringing unconditional belonging to humanity would most definitely be humbling practices too.

A BRIDGE BETWEEN HEAVEN AND EARTH

For Immanuel Kant, the genius was the artist who had the natural talent to bring divine beauty into the world.[23] For Martin Heidegger, the poet was someone who could unconceal the holiness lost in the everyday through language.[24] These artists and poets bridge the heavens with the earth through creativity. Through this process of divine creation, these individuals form yardsticks for other human beings to measure against. This measure, however, is not for comparing superiority, counter to what our modern competitive society would think. Instead, this measure exists to support humanity's humility and our faith in the unknown.

Why? Because if artists can create beauty from a divine source, and poets can express holiness through language, other humans like them must also have the power to bring heaven to earth. If any human being can have such power, then in the case of a landscape creative (for example, a gardener, a designer, a landscape architect) who works with physical landscapes that literally bridge the sky with the earth, what do they specifically do? Since people speak of "soul-searching" and escaping from "soul-sucking" jobs, implying that souls are transferable and retrievable between persons and situations, why not consider the landscape creative as the guardian of a landscape's soul? With a bit of faith, we could take a leap into the unknown to see poignant landscapes as places that move souls. With a bigger leap, we can imagine that the essence of a soul can be transferred between a person to a landscape, and in reciprocity, from a landscape to another person.

But what if we are afraid of heights and are hesitating at the cliff's edge? Well, the spiritual advice is to jump anyway since there is no point in reaching for rational explanations to decipher life's mysteries so that we can validate our own desperate desires to leap into the unknown. The soft landing into heaven on earth cannot be seen beforehand, but its invisible call is its proof of existence. But be reassured that things are often imperceptible not because they do not exist, but because of the way they are perceived. There may be many ways to see a landscape, but to see a poignant one, we need to take the leap into the depths of who we are inside first. And there we'll find that poignant landscapes move our souls because both we and landscape come from the same source. Among this landscape is also the origins of a poignant piece of artwork or poetry. Therefore, the landscape creative is meant to take on a similar role as the genius artist and poet—the role of creating moments of faith for humanity with landscapes that can touch our souls and inspire us to keep on trusting.

Taking Pain Off the Pedestal

Now I know why the trees change colour

Now I know why the trees change colour
The poplars in the distance glimmer and glisten
Twinkling, twinkling, like magic
The branches of the copper beech sway up and down
Like the arms of a pianist
Dancing in the wind composed of sweet music.

Swish, swish, swish...

Now I know why the trees lose their leaves
They fall, being taken over by the force of the wind
Teaching me to flow along with life
They fall, drifting through the air
Teaching me how to let go and descend with grace.

Landing on the ground is not a shame
Because the trees have been collecting sunshine
All summer long, to cover the ground
With a mass of golden blankets
To warm my heart, in preparation for winter.

LEARNING TO LOVE IS
LEARNING TO BE LOVED

When a person feels belonging, they feel nurtured, and like a plant in the right environment, they flourish. When a person doesn't feel that they belong, they do not feel nurtured, and like a plant forced to grow in an unsuitable environment, they have trouble flourishing. Considering that much of our human civilizations and social structures have been built on psychological environments of unnourishing fear and shame, collective belonging inevitably has become a challenge for us contemporary humans. The growing nature-connection movement attempts to get us back in touch with our roots as natural beings, but something pivotal blocks our way—the fact that relationships are always mutual.

Traditional discourse in environmental ethics argues that humans should learn to love nature in order to be better stewards of the land. But if we do not feel nurtured, regardless of the reasons, what do we have to give in this relationship? Environmental education scholars Jani Pulkki, Bo Dahlin, and Veli-Matti Varri suggest that we need a "biophilia revolution."[25] Rather than focus on a love for nature, they suggest that modern people should instead focus on healing our biophobia: our fear of the nature external to us and the fear of the nature within us.

Pulkki et.al suggest the practice of embodiment as a pedagogy to reconnect with the nature inside and outside of us. Yet, as someone who has been trained to support myself and others with embodiment experiences in natural environments, I still come across a message from my own body—the empathic body that has "absorbed" much of my family's, our society's, and our collective humanity's pain: *How can people become more in tune with their bodies if the first thing they encounter within their bodies is the repressed pain of not-belonging?*

Therefore, I suggest that the "biophilia revolution" needs an extra turn. The reason why humans do not know how to love nature is not just because we are afraid of nature. Yes, there are many potential reasons for us to be afraid of nature's uncontrollability...the risks of being chased by tigers...being bitten by poisonous snakes...being hit by lightning...having our homes overturned by a tornado...encountering a psychopathic serial killer...being born into a country ruled by the twisted cruelty of a narcissistic dictator...or the many other threats of human and non-human nature. But many of us are also afraid of something we desperately want from nature. As beings so used to judgmental social environments and being prone to question our existential belongingness, collectively, humans are also afraid of Nature's love for us—to be witnessed without judgment and to be offered unconditional love. Fundamentally, to learn to love nature, we must reconcile the question of our own lovability: *How can we be worthy of such love when our own nature has been so destructive, cruel, and violent to ourselves and to Mother Earth herself?*

Consequently, my intuitive "solution" for a just and sustainable world isn't about learning to love nature and attempting to gain equality through redistributing fairness. Instead, the path to reconciliation is to learn to be loved by nature and to embody the essence of equality and non-judgement as self-forgiveness for the cruelty of our species' woundedness and as the honouring of the innocent ones who succumbed to the inhumanity of these wounds. And if we are to commit to the narrative that we are nature, in accordance with the nature-connection movement and environmental advocacy, then learning to let nature love us and learning to embody nature's unconditional love is also about learning to be self-compassionate in the process of remembering how to love ourselves.

MAKING SOUL AND CHOOSING MAGIC

Even though the debate over whether souls exist has been an ongoing one in religion, philosophy, science, and popular culture since the birth of modern thought, I have, nevertheless, been disappointed to know that not everyone believes in souls. This debate, in my opinion, is totally misguided since the relevance of soul is based on *making* meaning rather than *finding* something of evidence in physical form. Believing in souls is a choice to instill meaning into life (to make soul) or to eradicate meaning from life (to make things soulless). The same analogy can be applied to poignant experiences, poignant landscapes, and magic.

Sometimes in life, we encounter teachings that tempt us to eradicate soul from something that was once soulful, for example, the advice to abandon a passion for an unfavourable but stable job, the pressure to settle for a partner despite the absence of love, or the guilt-trip for appreciating the blessings we've been given because of other people's misfortunes. During these testing times of our soul's strength, the only way out is to surrender to faith. This surrendering is an intentional process of allowing the mind's limitations to subside in order to allow the unfamiliar to enter. When I had once felt defeated by the guilt for "romanticizing" landscapes and the shame for being human in what has been ethically advocated as an ecologically and socially "damaged" world, an antidotal reassurance came from David Abram's notion of magic. Sleight-of-hand magicians and traditional shamans, according to Abram, create magic by being mediators of perception.[26] In the case of a performance, magic occurs only when both the magician and the audience willingly participate with their imaginations. Alternatively, those who do not want to participate, inevitably, would be entranced by logical explanations and analyses, such as hidden wires or mirrors.

Therefore, both magic and soul are for those who want to believe. In the same vein, the enchantment of poignant landscapes is for those who want to be enchanted by the world. To see magic, live soulfully, and be moved by a landscape, one must be courageous enough to dispel other people's disenchantment and be persistent enough to continuously choose a path of enchantment even when life looks otherwise. Fortunately, as human beings, we can always gain insights about making soulful choices by contemplating on our lives' finitude, since to be alive is at the same time to be mortal and to be aware of human limitedness. Life's preciousness, which can often be felt as poignant moments, is only made possible by its counterpart of death.

Landscapes exhibit this dichotomy of life and death since all living beings eventually die. Constructed elements, also, will deteriorate—sometimes beyond the life of humans, showcasing the limit to human mortality even more. But when a landscape expresses lessons of life and death, the experience often manifests as a beautiful yet painful moment, for example, the poignant beauty of cherry blossoms falling in the spring. We learn from the cherry blossoms that even though they do not last forever, they will still bloom marvellously when the time is right for them to do so.

The time between birth and death for a flower is a chance to flourish. Likewise, the time between birth and death for a human is also the opportunity to flourish. Despite our natural dread of death, we know that none of us, in our material forms, will last forever. Therefore, the process of life, the experience of flourishing, is the value of life itself. This journey of life is an interlocked process that occurs between flower/person and their environment. From Odysseus to Harry Potter to Anne of Green Gables, the Hero(ine)'s Journey cannot exist without their beloved landscapes. Neither can our own Life Journey. During this time of existence in our corporeal forms, we are placed in a world with other beings in tangible and intangible landscapes. This sojourn is our temporary stay on Earth as human beings but also our timeless engagement with the truth of our divinity. Each piece of landscape we encounter teaches us a lesson about this duality.

As a philosopher and a student of spirituality, I am inevitably drawn to the enigma of our intangible landscapes, but ironically, by turning the formlessness of these poignant landscapes into the perceptibility of a research project, I've discovered that I do not need to pilgrimage for poignant landscapes anymore. In the process of just *being* within a landscape, I've found that poignant landscape experiences have simplified and diversified for me. For example, extremely windy places can fascinate me; arduous hikes on park trails sometimes seem masochistic yet memorable; ordinary visits to neighbourhood parks are welcoming and healing; and sitting on my balcony can feel oddly comforting. Rather than a spectator longing to be embraced by the landscape, I have learned to become a participant in the landscape and allow myself to be embraced by it. Learning to be aware of my senses, the landscape's elements, my relationship with the landscape, and that I belonged in it, landscape has also become an acknowledged and respected counterpart of my life.

LEARNING FROM FLOWERS

What if the flowers listened to that evil voice
That said being admired is bad
And sharing beauty is vain,
What world would we live in?

Imagine if the moon didn't shine,
The sun hid its radiance,
And the stars decided not to glitter,
Could we still survive here on this Earth?

I hear the flowers shouting in their chipper voices,
Don't listen to that ugly voice of the sea monster
Who doesn't want you to return home
To shine your light.

Listen to us, we know the truth
This world cannot exist without our beauty
Because we are the mirrors of your heart
Ready to bloom.

BEYOND THE GATEKEEPER

Identifying with titles and names does matter in society but they also do not have to. A name like any other word, can animate the thing or being it signifies. For example, Mother Earth and Father Sky are found with different names in different cultures: as Prithvi Mata and Dyaus Pita (Hinduism), Gaia and Uranus (Ancient Greek), and Wākea and Papahānaumoku (Hawaiian mythology). Humanity's greatest forces such as love, truth, and strife are also enlivened in Ancient Greek mythology as God Eros, Goddess Alethea, and Goddess Eris. Nature, as primordial elements of the world or as humans' way of life, is animated through names. But is a "rose" always a "rose"? (In reference to Gertrude Stein's commonly known quote, "a rose is a rose is a rose," meaning that things are what they are.) Perhaps not: my name is meaningless without my story, but I am not meaningless without my name.

A real-life story of a landscape architect's encounter with an Indigenous man at a National Reconciliation Gathering in Ottawa, Canada provides anecdotal context to my contemplative thoughts about names. During a break, the man comes up to the landscape architect and asks, "Who are you?" But instead of telling him her name, she instinctively replies, "I'm a landscape architect." The man says in response, "Oh, I'm also a landscape architect. I take care of the land." While this encounter illuminated the purpose of the landscape architect's calling into the profession, this story also begs the question of societal labels. In Ontario, Canada, the profession of landscape architecture is legislated under a Title Act, meaning legally, one cannot call themself a landscape architect without membership to the professional association, and yet, this man, who did not work as a professional landscape architect, embodied the archetypal essence of a landscape architect and unabashedly referred to himself as one.

This story reminds me of a scene from Antoine de Saint-Exupéry's classic story of *The Little Prince*. In the scene, the Little Prince asks the flowers he meets in a garden on Earth, "Who are you?"[27] The flowers, which look exactly like his nameless flower from Asteroid B-612, reply, "We're roses." At first, the Little Prince is disappointed that his flower was not the only one of her kind in the whole universe and mistakes the interchangeableness of his beloved flower with the 500 roses he meets on Earth, but soon, he realizes that his rose was not the same as these roses. He and his rose have "tamed" each other and have bonded through times of nurturing.

The roses on Earth in the story identify as roses while the rose on Asteroid B-612 identifies as one-and-only. In times of uncertainty, I also ask myself, who (rather than what) do I identify as? And in reciprocity, I ask you, who do you identify as? How do our names, our titles, and our words alter the world? Can we feel our commonality if we remain fully identified as our titular roles in our sub-groups? And then, can we care for the world's common grounds if we do not feel our world's commonality because of our titles? The answer to these questions, I presume, will remain vague. But if "anything essential is invisible to the eyes," as noted by Saint-Exupéry, then all that matters is the heart's intention.[28] With this intention, I trust that our words can find their way to speak to the world, for the collective, and in honour of ourselves, with or without our labels.

But be forewarned, as our language can change the way we relate to ourselves and our environments, because the alphabet, as a collection of mental symbols, "short-circuits" our relationship with the land to which we belong.[29] Comparatively, if the alphabet is the gatekeeper to (phonetic) language, then human identity is the gatekeeper to the soul. Maybe he or she guards the land of the invisible, and maybe, sometimes, we want the gatekeeper out of the way. I have yet to fully reconcile this idea, but as parts of my identity die, I sometimes find myself mourning for them. However, certainly, I am ready for regeneration.

TIME TO TAKE PAIN OFF THE PEDESTAL

Originating from two different human civilizations over a gap of more than 2,000 years, Romanticism and Daoism (referring to the philosophy, not the religion) have some distinct similarities. Both philosophical movements were born out of social discontent, emphasized a return to nature, valued personal expression, and acknowledged life's paradoxes. However, being a Romantic is much more painful than being a Daoist, because to be Romantic also means to put the pain of not-belonging up on a pedestal. That is why, I often describe myself as a Romantic learning to be a Daoist.

Marshall Berman's quote, "to be fully modern is to be anti-modern," describes the essence of Romanticism.[30] Often chastened as too sentimental and idealistic, the Romantic chooses to forgo established structures of authority in search of realities expressed in personal experiences.[31] Like the archetypal orphaned child who is simultaneously traumatized by the world yet intuitively cognizant of the universe's purity from their unborn state, the Romantic remains anxious and skeptical of the potential for a reunion with a loving caregiver. So, while the Romantic yearns to be united with nature, as a perpetual outsider,[32] they can only examine the world at a distance. As a bystander to the scenes of life, landscapes (through Western art's perspective) become the constructed images to represent this incomplete unity with nature and with self.

On the other hand, Daoism recognizes the polarity of human objectivity and subjectivity and the yin and yang polarity in all things. While the historical existence of the author Laozi has been disputed, the legend of *Daodejing*'s origin as a departure gift from Laozi in his withdrawal as a royal court official places the classical text as a piece of political disillusionment turned sacred wisdom. Therefore, unlike the orphaned child who yearns and fears unity, the enlightened Daoist recognizes that beneath the chaos is already unity. Accordingly, the layering of a landscape in traditional Daoist paintings reminds us that truth is a discovery to be revealed through a process of un-concealing.[33] The uncertainty of nature and human life is to be accepted because what is divine cannot be found outside of us as the saviour to redeem our sense of unbelonging. Instead, what is sacred is found in our awareness that we already exist exactly as who we are and where we are amidst these uncertainties.

Like the Romantics who tried to mitigate the pain of incompleteness by celebrating difficult emotions, I also learned to value the pain of being human. But in curating this book, I also realized how much I had worshipped pain. Knowing that pain and beauty are two sides of the same coin, I appreciated the fact that even if most of the world was ignorant of the beauty of divinity, pain still exists as the divine connection that holds us together. Yet paradoxically, pain is both the key to our healing and the reason that we have yet to be healed. But rather than allowing pain to be transformed into beauty in the liminal state of poignancy, I often mistook poignancy as equivalent to both beauty *and* pain.

As my teenage self had already known, the secrets of the world stay stored in the body of the Thinker until someone dares to free them from eternal suffering. So, may I ask, what kind of pain lives in your body as a result of your Thinker? Or perhaps, this pain comes from the collective Thinker of humanity. Yet, who will be so daring to free this Thinker from its suffering than the Lover herself? But to master the love of wisdom is not only to succeed in finding the beauty of truth like the Romantics did. This mastery is also about knowing when to take pain off the pedestal so that love, pain, and beauty can participate in the world together. So, while pain and beauty are not equivalent, the beauty *of* pain is that pain was always meant to be free.

POIGNANT LANDSCAPES

Poignant landscapes
Are they the windows out to the land's soul?
No, they are the windows into our own souls
Peace, serenity, hope
Love
The landscape embraces me and my heart
And tells me, everything is ok
I am with you, we are together
In sharing the beauty of the world.

ENDNOTES

1. Victor Turner, *The Ritual Process: Structure and Anti-Structure*, (Ithaca: Cornell University Press, 1969).

2. Treanor and Brendan Sweetman, "Gabriel (-Honoré) Marcel" in *The Stanford Encyclopedia of Philosophy*, ed. Edward N. Zalta (Metaphysics Research Lab, Stanford University, 2016), https://plato.stanford.edu/archives/win2016/entries/marcel/.

3. Tim Edensor, "Aurora Landscapes: Affective Atmospheres of Light and Dark" in *Conversations with Landscape*, ed. by Karl Benediktsson and Katrín Anna Lund, (Farnham, Surrey: Ashgate, 2010).

4. Yi Fu Tuan, *Topophilia: A Study of Environmental Perception, Attitudes, and Values*, Morningside ed. (New York: Columbia University Press, 1990).

5. Tuan, *Topophilia*; Gina Crandell, *Nature Pictorialized: 'The View' in Landscape History*, (Baltimore: Johns Hopkins University Press, 1993).

6. Joanna Macy, "Working through Environmental Despair" in *Ecopychology: Restoring the Earth, Healing the Mind*, ed. Theodore Roszak, Mary E. Gomes, and Allen D. Kanner, (San Francisco: Sierra Club Books, 1995).

7. Andy Fisher, *Radical Ecopsychology: Psychology in the Service of Life*, 2nd ed., (New York: SUNY Press, 2013).

8. Robert J. Richards, *The Romantic Conception of Life: Science and Philosophy in the Age of Goethe*, (Chicago: University of Chicago Press, 2002).

9. Fisher, *Radical Ecopsychology*.

10. "Poignant" in *Online Etymology Dictionary*, accessed 15 January 2020, https://www.etymonline.com/word/poignant.

11. Stephen Jenkinson, "So Who Are the Dying to You? Who Are the Dead?" in *Die Wise: A Manifesto for Sanity and Soul*, (Berkeley: North Atlantic Books, 2015).

12. Carl Jung, *Psychology of the Unconscious*, trans. Beatrice M. Hinkle, (Project Gutenberg E-books, 2021), https://www.gutenberg.org/ebooks/65903.

13. James Hillman, *The Dream and the Underworld*, (New York: Harper & Row, 1979).

14. Martin Heidegger, *Poetry, Language, Thought*, trans. Albert Hofstadter, (New York: Harper Perennial, 1971), 218.

15. Frederick Law Olmsted, "Yosemite and the Mariposa Grove: A Preliminary Report," 1865, http://www.yosemite.ca.us/library/olmsted/report.html.

16. Crandell, *Nature Pictorialized*.

17. Michael Sullivan, *Symbols of Eternity: The Art of Landscape Painting in China*, (Stanford: Stanford University Press, 1979).

18. Jay Goulding, "John O'Neill's Phenomenology: The Copper Rule," in *John O'Neill's body of work re-Joyced*, ed. Mauro Buccheri and Livy Visano, (Toronto: Founders' College, York University, 2016).

19. Jay Goulding, "Visceral Manifestation: Chinese Philosophy and Western Phenomenology." In *Chinese Philosophy and Trends of the 21st Century*, Vol. 4, ed. Fang Keli, (Beijing: Commercial Press, 2003).

20. Norris B. Johnson, "Geomancy, Sacred Geometry, and the Idea of a Garden: Tenryu-Ji Temple, Kyoto, Japan," *Journal of Garden History*, Vol 9, Issue 1 (1989): 1–19, 2.

21. Camelia Nakagawara, "The Japanese Garden for the Mind: The 'Bliss' of Paradise Transcended," *Stanford Journal of East Asian Affairs*, Vol. 4, Issue 2 (2004): 83–102.

22. Nakagawara, "The Japanese Garden for the Mind"; Barry Stephenson, "The Kōan as Ritual Performance," *Journal of the American Academy of Religion* Vol. 73, Issue 2 (2005): 475–96.

23. Immanual Kant, *The Critique of Judgement*, trans. James Creed Meredith (Oxford: Clarendon Press, 1952).

24. Heidegger, *Poetry, Language, Thought.*

25. Jani Pulkki, Bo Dahlin and Veli-Matti Värri, "Environmental Education as a Lived-Body Experience? A Contemplative Pedagogy Perspective," in *Journal of Philosophy of Education*, Vol. 50, No. 4 (2016).

26. David Abram, *The Spell of the Sensuous: Perception and Language in a More-Than-Human World*, (New York: Vintage Books, 1997).

27. Antoine de Saint-Exupéry, *The Little Prince*, trans. Richard Howard, (San Diego: Harcourt, 2000), 54.

28. Saint-Exupéry, *The Little Prince*, 63.

29. Abram, *The Spell of the Sensuous*; Fisher, *Radical Ecopsychology*.

30. Marshall Berman, *All That is Solid Melts Into Air: The Experience of Modernity*, (New York: Penguin Books, 1988).

31. Neil Evernden, *The Natural Alien: Human Kind and Environment*, (Toronto: University of Toronto Press, 1985).

32. Evernden, *The Natural Alien*.

33. Van Thi Diep, "The Landscape of the Void: Truth and Magic in Chinese Landscape Painting," *Journal of Visual Art Practice*, Vol. 16, Issue 1 (2017): 77-86.

ACKNOWLEDGEMENTS

Although this book was published several years after I completed my doctoral degree, I continue to be thankful for the following people and institutions from my graduate school days who supported me on my landscape journey: my PhD committee members—Laura Taylor, Peter Timmerman, and Martin Holland; my teachers of ecopsychology and phenomenology—Andy Fisher and Jay Goulding; the Social Sciences and Humanities Research Council and the Landscape Architecture Canada Foundation for research funding; and the landscape architects who participated in the research.

If my dissertation was the product of what my mind had gained from poignant landscapes, then the last few years of life have been the embodied practice of this wisdom. As we all know, things are easier said (and written) than done. So, I would also like to acknowledge my forest therapy guide trainers, fellow trainees and walk participants, the forests, parks, and gardens, as well as the beings that lived there, who together held space for me to renew my trust in the power of landscapes and my inherent belonging in them.

ABOUT THE AUTHOR

Van Thi Diep, who was born in Vietnam to ethnically Chinese parents and raised in Canada, has long been familiar with the imperfections of social identities. Often finding herself in the liminal space of "in-betweens" such as structure and creativity, thinking and feeling, logic and intuition, she finds resonance in indefinable subjects such as landscapes, spirituality, arts & crafts, and ecopsychology. Van Thi holds a PhD in environmental studies from York University, and as a retired landscape architect turned environmental philosopher and certified forest therapy guide, she sees landscapes as the bridge between humanity's inner nature and the world's outer nature. Considering that her name in its original Chinese form means *leaf rhyme poem*, Van Thi is grateful to embody this title in sharing the poetic beauty of nature with the world.

***

www.vtdiep.ca

Milton Keynes UK
Ingram Content Group UK Ltd.
UKHW052124250224
438371UK00006B/91/J